Chin Na Fa

Chin Na Fa

Traditional Chinese Submission Grappling

Liu Jinsheng & Zhao Jiang

Translated by

Tim Cartmell

BLUE SNAKE BOOKS

Berkeley, California

Published by Blue Snake Books

Blue Snake Books
are distributed by
North Atlantic Books
P.O. Box 12327
Berkeley, California 94712

Interior text/art from original Chinese edition
of Chin Na Fa.
Cover and book design by Brad Greene
Printed in the United States of America

Blue Snake Books' publications are available through most bookstores. For further information, call 800-337-2665 or visit our websites at www.northatlanticbooks.com or www.bluesnakebooks.com.

Substantial discounts on bulk quantities are available to corporations, professional associations, and other organizations. For details and discount information, contact our special sales department.

PLEASE NOTE: The creators and publishers of this book are not and will not be responsible, in any way whatsoever, for any improper use made by anyone of the information contained in this book. All use of the aforementioned information must be made in accordance with what is permitted by law, and any damage liable to be caused as a result thereof will be the exclusive responsibility of the user. In addition, he or she must adhere strictly to the safety rules contained in the book, both in training and in actual implementation of the information presented herein. This book is intended for use in conjunction with ongoing lessons and personal training with an authorized expert. It is not a substitute for formal training. It is the sole responsibility of every person planning to train in the techniques described in this book to consult a licensed physician in order to obtain complete medical information on his or her personal ability and limitations. The instructions and advice printed in this book are not in any way intended as a substitute for medical, mental, or emotional counseling with a licensed physician or healthcare provider.

Library of Congress Cataloging-in-Publication Data

Liu, Jinsheng.
  [Chin na fa. English]
  Chin na fa : traditional Chinese submission grappling techniques / by Liu Jinsheng and Zhao Jiang ; translated by Timothy Cartmell.
      p. cm.
  Summary: "Chin Na Fa is translation of a classic text on Chinese grappling methods, originally published in Chinese in 1936, written by experts of the Chinese method as a training manual for the Police Academy of Zheijiang province"—Provided by publisher.
  ISBN-13: 978-1-58394-185-0 (trade paper)
  ISBN-10: 1-58394-185-1 (trade paper)
  1. Martial arts. 2. Hand-to-hand fighting. 3. Police training. 4. Self defense for police. I. Zhao, Jiang. II. Cartmell, Tim. III. Title. IV. Title: Traditional Chinese submission grappling techniques.
  GV1101.L58513 2007
  796.815'5—dc22

                                                                    2007008179
                                                                           CIP

1 2 3 4 5 6 7 8 9 UNITED 12 11 10 09 08 07

About This Book

Chin Na Fa was written by Liu Jinsheng and Zhao Jiang and published in 1936. The work was edited by the Zhejiang Province Police Officers Academy and distributed by the Shanghai Commerce Publishers.

Liu Jinsheng was born in Shandong Province. According to his foreword in this book: "When I was young, my grandfather, Fang Chengxun, gave me a copy of an ancient manuscript containing the secret techniques of Chin Na Fa. I practiced according to the illustrations for three years, but I failed to comprehend the great value of the work. Only after training for over twenty years in various arts with the northern master Wang Ziping and more than twenty other teachers, did I begin to understand this ancient manuscript's worth as a unique transmission of a true art."

The techniques of Chin Na Fa include strikes to vital points, joint locks, and throws. The art emphasizes techniques that separate the tendons, misalign the bones, interrupt the opponent's breath, and damage vital points. Clever techniques are favored over brute force; consequently, these skills have been of great use to military and police forces.

In the introduction to the book the author writes, "The original names of this art were the Art of Separating the Tendons, the Art of Adhering Grips and Takedowns, the Art of Filing the Bones, and the Art of Seizing and Grasping. In modern times, the name

Chin Na Fa

Art of Seizing and Grasping (Chin Na Shu) has been chosen as the standard. The art includes seventy-two techniques." In the martial arts world, there are many references to the so-called thirty-six main cavities and the seventy-two minor cavities. In Chin Na Fa, there is also often reference to the "thirty-six techniques," "seventy-two techniques," or "one-hundred-and-eight techniques." These correspond to ancient ideas of celestial and terrestrial formations and should not be taken as the literal number of techniques in the art of Chin Na Fa.

The book contains a foreword by Zhao Lungwen, the preface, the introduction, and the main text. The main text contains eight sections: Section One covers techniques applied to the head; Section Two, techniques applied to the neck; Section Three, techniques applied to the shoulder; Section Four, techniques applied to the chest, ribs, and back; Section Five, techniques applied to the waist; Section Six, techniques applied to the arms and wrists; Section Seven, techniques applied to the fingers; and Section Eight, techniques applied to the legs and the feet.

Table of Contents

PORTRAIT OF THE AUTHOR, LIU JINSHENG

Foreword

Mr. Liu Jinsheng studied in Shandong province. He has been in Zhejiang for six years and has students from both the east and west regions of the province. Despite his success, Liu Jinsheng has not become arrogant—in his spare time, he continues to research his art with friends to improve his skills.

I am in charge of training the police in Zhejiang province. I feel strongly that if police officers are not thoroughly trained in the martial skills best used in the apprehension of gangsters, brigands, and those who disturb the peace, they cannot fulfill their obligations of duty. Whenever I discuss these matters with Mr. Liu and ask him to illustrate direct and efficient techniques for use in police matters, he explains the skills of Chin Na. There are many martial arts in our country that teach ways to injure an opponent; however, it is against regulation for police officers to use such methods in their work. Police officers are soldiers of peace and must not injure others. Chin Na is unsurpassed as an art that will allow one to control another without inflicting injury. In this book, the author has meticulously laid out his teachings to great effect. Those involved in peacekeeping now have a work to research and examine. This book is a great contribution to society.

—Zhao Lungwen

Translator's Preface

This work represents primary source material of ancient combat techniques designed to restrain, control, injure, or kill an opponent in hand-to-hand combat. The intent of this translation is to provide authentic historical documentation for martial arts techniques that have been modified for use today in both competition and self-defense. The reader will notice the frequent references to the potential for serious injury and lethality of the methods taught. The book was written and published in a time of occupation and war, when the threat of lethal hand-to-hand combat was an ever-present reality for soldiers, those involved in law enforcement, and very often for the ordinary citizen.

From such techniques and methods modern techniques of self-defense and combat sport competition have evolved. It is important to realize that the Chin Na techniques presented here can be practiced safely and applied practically in most instances without causing permanent injury or death. Joint locks, pressure techniques, chokes, and strangles may be applied at various levels of force. Enough force may be applied to control and restrain an assailant without causing excessive damage. More serious situations may call for more serious levels of force that we are in no way condoning outside of this context.

Chin Na-based techniques have several great advantages over percussion-based (striking) techniques. The first advantage is that joint locks and chokes are based on leverage; with correctly applied leverage a smaller fighter may amplify their force many times over, providing a method of overcoming a much stronger and heavier opponent. Another advantage of Chin Na-based techniques is that they may be practiced in a realistic manner, at full speed against full resistance, without injuring the training partner. When caught in a joint lock or choke, the partner can signal defeat (most commonly by "tapping out") and the partner applying the technique stops applying force. Partners only concede submission when a technique is on the verge of doing serious harm or causing unconsciousness, so one is assured the technique is really effective. Training in this manner, realistic skills are developed with a minimal chance of injury. Finally, in an actual fight, Chin Na-based techniques may be applied at various levels of force. The Chin Na-trained defender may apply only enough force to control the attacker and remove the threat of attack. In more dangerous situations the defender may break or dislocate a limb or joint, or choke the attacker into unconsciousness. Striking techniques are more reliant on size and strength over leverage, cannot be trained full force (for fear of injuring the training partner), and must be applied full force (lacking levels of force) in a real confrontation.

Readers familiar with other styles of martial arts that include leverage based, joint locking, choking, and strangling techniques will see many similar or identical techniques in this work. Practitioners of Judo, Brazilian Jiu-Jitsu, Sambo, and the various styles of submission wrestling will find many techniques they are familiar with from their respective styles. These types of techniques, whatever their source of origin, have proven most useful not only in self-defense but also in realistic combat sports competition. For example, the variations of the arm bars and many of the chokes and holds are found in the above-mentioned styles of combat sport.

More specifically, many choking techniques found in the classical Chin Na repertoire are found in other popular grappling styles. "Pinching the Arm from the Front" is also known as a "Guillotine" choke in Brazilian Jiu-Jitsu; the "Pinching with the Arm from the Rear" technique is the famous "Rear Naked Choke," a common submission hold found in Judo, Jiu-Jitsu and submissions wrestling, as well as being one of the most common finishing holds used in mixed martial arts competition; the "Front Throat Lock" is the "Cross Choke" of Judo and Brazilian Jiu-Jitsu.

Many Chin Na joint locking techniques are also found in the grappling arts of different cultures. The "Small Entwining" wrist lock is known as "Nikyo" in Aikido; "Bend the Elbow and Break the Arm" is the "Entangled Arm Lock" (ude garami) of Judo. "Tearing the Wing" is known in Western Wrestling as a "Chicken Wing"; "Mounting the Horse" is a variation of the "Jujigatame" or cross armbar found in Judo and Brazilian Jiu-Jitsu, and is also a common submission in mixed martial arts events; "Sitting on the Leg" is analogous to the "Knee Bar" found in Sambo and submission wrestling.

Any study or use of martial art techniques should be done directly with a qualified master in that art, and this book is not a substitute for that, but an opportunity for the study of the origins of techniques we use today.

Chin Na Fa is a direct translation of an original Chinese document, including the images connected to the text. Readers are encouraged to remember the social climate, political situation, and times in which it was published. Besides being a collection of excellent, time-tested techniques of hand-to-hand fighting, the work provides a window into the mind-set of trained martial artists in a turbulent time.

A special thanks to Mr. Liu Jinsheng for his contribution of the original text: www.lionbooks.com.tw.

Author's Preface

In recent times, those who discuss preparation for war emphasize the weapons of the army, navy, and air force, overlooking the traditional martial arts of China. Since the defeat of the Yi He Group in the Ching dynasty, traditional martial arts have developed a bad reputation, and those with real martial arts skills have become reluctant to share their knowledge. The result has been that the image of the martial hero has been replaced by the image of the "sick man of Asia." For the last several decades, the outside world has viewed my country in this manner.

Since the Meiji Restoration, our eastern neighbor Japan has risen in status to become one of the strongest nations in the world. Most people believe Japan has modeled itself after Europe and the West, not knowing that long before the Meiji Restoration, the country was most greatly influenced by Bushido (Way of the Warrior) and the Great Spirit of Cooperation. And if we research the origins of Bushido, we find its origin in China. During the Ming dynasty, Chen Yuanbin traveled to Japan and taught the skills of seizing and locking as well as wrestling. His students practiced assiduously, and the government promoted the art under the new name of judo. Judo was actively promoted until it was practiced by the general populace throughout the country. Slowly, the people were transformed into the fearsome and skilled fighters we know of the country today.

Simply talking about saving our country without promoting China's traditional martial arts is not enough to shake up the apathetic spirit of our people. In recent years, the central government has begun to promote traditional martial arts, and every province has established martial arts training halls. Besides Chinese wrestling, the most popular arts are the Shaolin and Wudang styles of kung fu, both of which have methods of solo practice. Yet the practical applications of these arts is a subject that is never breached. Those who have practiced these arts twenty or thirty years have never defeated anyone who has practiced Western boxing or judo. Why is this? It is because the practitioners of Shaolin and Wudang styles only pay attention to the beauty of their forms—they lack practical methods and spirit and have lost the true transmissions of their ancestors. Hence, our martial arts are viewed by outsiders merely as rigorous dancing.

When the ancients practiced any type of martial art, sparring and drilling techniques were one and the same. Once a fight started, techniques flowed in sequence, six or seven at a time, never giving the opponent a chance to win. In the Ming dynasty, men such as Qi Jiguang and Yu Dayou advocated this type of realistic practice and opposed any empty practice done for the sake of appearance. This is why these men have proud reputations in history.

Today the scientific method is employed the world over. All disciplines seek to further refine their techniques. Only China fails to improve its traditional martial arts over time, and even our past knowledge is being lost. Because the ancients would not transmit their knowledge readily, fewer and fewer people carry on their traditions and much of their knowledge has been lost. This is a great pity.

When I was young, my grandfather, Fang Chengxun, gave me a copy of an ancient manuscript containing the secret techniques of Chin Na Fa. I practiced according to the illustrations for three years, but I failed to comprehend the great value of the work. Only after training for over twenty years in various arts with the northern master Wang Ziping and more than twenty other teachers, did I begin to understand this ancient manuscript's worth as a unique transmission of a true art. I hope my presentation of this work proves to have merit and provides the reader with information worthy of further research.

—Liu Jinsheng

Zhejiang Province Police Officers Academy, 1935

Introduction

The original names of Chin Na Fa were the "Art of Separating the Tendons," the "Art of Adhering Grips and Takedowns," the "Art of Filing the Bones," and the "Method of Seizing and Grasping." The ancient manuscripts refer to this art as "Disha Shou." It was the only art used for national defense and personal protection, as it is especially suited for use by police and military forces.

There are seventy-two techniques total. The techniques included in this book are meticulously explained. The Chinese characters used have been chosen for their clarity and simplicity. The reader will understand the meaning of the text immediately and will be able to follow the instructions provided for practice.

This art is purely for real-life application, and it is devoid of useless or showy techniques. Trying to practice alone will prove ineffective; students must practice the techniques in pairs. During practice, students must apply the techniques correctly—the "opponent" should feel pain at the moment of contact. Be careful not to use too much force when applying techniques, as there is a real danger of torn tendons and broken bones. Of course, in actual fighting situations one should not hold back.

Whether you are a civilian or a military or police officer, if you devote sufficient time to practicing the techniques contained in this book, they will become yours. Once these techniques have been mastered, the fate of your opponents will lie in your hands. The art can be tested at any time: you will never be in danger.

This art contains techniques that can kill an enemy, snap his tendons, break his bones, or render him unconscious. During hand-to-hand combat with foreign enemies, these techniques will be the key to victory.

If you are arresting a suspect and run into resistance, the techniques of Chin Na Fa can be applied to immobilize the suspect without inflicting great injury. Suspects can be rendered unconscious or captured in holds and later revived or released when safely in custody. (Holds must not be applied for more than two hours.)

The techniques of this art, once mastered, may be applied by women as well as by the weak to overcome stronger opponents.

The techniques are all applied using coordinated strength, never brute force. Daily practice will make the body as pliable as cotton, with a balance of hard and soft. One will cultivate a type of resilient and springy force—a body with strength in the midst of flexibility.

Practitioners of this art must concurrently train and combine four types of skills: attacking vital points, locking, throwing, and striking. This type of training will produce the highest level of skill in a practitioner, and he or she will prevail even if confronted by an enemy of enormous strength. However, one must devote adequate time and effort to training, and take the training to heart to acquire real skill.

It is the nature of humans engaged in hand-to-hand conflict to throw a few blows and then immediately close in to grapple. It is in such close-quarter conditions that the techniques presented here can best be used. Students should make careful note of this.

The techniques of Chin Na Fa are the most refined of all the combat systems. This art has been kept hidden for a long time, almost to the point of being lost for good. I have now made this art available to the public. This book is an offering from the past to the people of my country.

Joint-locking techniques are the focus of this book, with the other three categories of techniques (attacking vital points, throws, and strikes) included within the techniques presented. The more complicated techniques are broken down into several steps, though in actual applications the steps must blend together to make one continuous action. The explanations in this book designate one partner as X and one as Y. This will aid instructors of military and police forces in teaching groups of trainees. If partners are divided into the roles of X and Y, the instructions will be easy to follow.

If practitioners have spent the required amount of time in serious training and have developed bravery, power, and skill, they will be able to apply their techniques in real world situations calmly, quickly, and decisively. Victory is assured. One must never forget the element of bravery. Without bravery, all other attributes are not worth mentioning.

Section **1**

Head Techniques

This chapter is included because in ancient times, people wore their hair long and the hair was often grabbed during an attack. Today, an opponent's hair may be too short to be grabbed, so these techniques will not always be applicable. The ancient manuscript contained these techniques, however, so they have been faithfully included here and are worth learning.

Number One: Front Hair Grab, Part One

This technique is applied when an opponent grabs your hair from the front.

Explanation

Y grabs X's hair from the front with his right hand. X immediately uses both hands to tightly press the back of Y's hand to the top of his head. X pulls back forcefully while simultaneously bending his head and body forward. As Y's arm is pulled straight and his wrist starts to bend, Y will fall forward forcefully. As Y falls, X must forcefully pull back and turn downward to his right. The sudden force will break Y's wrist.

Figure 1-1: Front Hair Grab, Part One

Number Two: Front Hair Grab, Part Two

This is an alternative technique that can be applied when an opponent grabs your hair from the front.

Explanation

This is the same scenario as illustrated in the previous technique: Y grabs X's hair from the front with his right hand. X grabs the back of Y's hand with his right hand, inserting his middle finger under Y's palm. At the same time, using his left hand, X grabs Y's forearm two or three inches below Y's wrist. X bends over and pulls backward, pulling Y's arm straight. When Y's wrist is bent slightly, X suddenly moves forward, stepping forward with his left foot. X presses his left elbow forward and downward from above with sudden force. This will break Y's wrist.

Figure 1-2: Front Hair Grab, Part Two

Number Three: Rear Hair Grab

This technique is applied when an opponent grabs your hair from the back.

Explanation

Y grabs X's hair from the rear with his right hand. X quickly reaches back with his right hand and firmly grabs the back of Y's hand. X forcefully pulls Y's hand to his right, while turning his body around to the right. As he turns, X uses his left hand to push Y's arm up, placing his hand just below the tip of Y's right elbow. X tilts his head back and pushes up suddenly with his left hand. Y will be forced to straighten his body. X continues to push under Y's elbow until the elbow breaks.

Figure 1-3: Rear Hair Grab

Number Four: Carrying the Lantern

This technique can be used when an opponent is either standing or lying on the ground.

Explanation

X uses the thumb and index finger of his right hand to grab Y's left earlobe. X 's right middle finger digs in forcefully behind the jaw just below Y's earlobe. X drives his finger inward and upward. At the same time, using his left hand, X grabs the top of Y's head just above his temple. X twists Y's head down and to the left. The hands coordinate, one pulling downward and the other pushing upward, until the twist causes an interruption of nerve transmissions and unconsciousness. To successfully apply this technique one must spend a considerable length of time strengthening the fingers.

Figure 1-4: Carrying the Lantern

Number Five: Grabbing the Face

This technique is applied when an opponent grabs the front of your chest.

Explanation

Y grabs the front of X's chest with his right hand. X immediately uses his left hand to press Y's hand to his chest. X moves his body back a little and pulls in his chest. X strikes downward suddenly with his right hand to the *qu chi* point (at the center of Y's forearm on the radial bone). The strike causes Y's body to lean forward. X now shoots his right hand forward and pinches the right side of Y's nose with his thumb as he grips the jaw below the ear with his four fingers. X squeezes Y's face hard. The pressure causes Y to freeze on the spot, unable to move, turn, or lift his hands or feet. This technique must be applied with great speed in order to be successful.

Figure 1-5: Grabbing the Face

Number Six: Removing the Helmet

This technique is applied when an opponent uses both hands to twist your head. After escaping, you counterattack.

Explanation

X grabs the hair on the back of Y's head with his right hand. At the same time, X grabs the area below the left side of Y's chin with his left hand. X bends his right elbow and adheres it to Y's chest. X presses into Y's chest with his right elbow as he pulls downward and inward with his right hand. X simultaneously pushes Y's chin outward and upward with his left hand. The force generated will cause Y's body to twist until his left arm is trapped behind X's back. Y will be unable to move away or strike X's groin. See Figure 1-6a.

Figure 1-6a: Removing the Helmet, Part One

If X is caught in the Removing the Helmet technique, he can escape by doing the following: Before the technique is completely locked, X must reach back behind his head quickly with his right hand

and grab Y's right wrist. As he grabs the wrist, X leans his body back. X then squats and sinks his left shoulder to below Y's right elbow. He rises up again, pushing upward from below Y's right elbow. As X pushes up below Y's right elbow, he turns his body to the right rear, which loosens the grip Y has on his chin. X then pulls Y's right wrist sharply down to his right with his right hand as he simultaneously presses up below Y's right elbow with his shoulder. X increases the force by standing up straight. The purpose of the technique is to break Y's elbow. See Figure 1-6b. If Y's elbow does not break, X can continue on to Part Three of the technique.

Figure 1-6b: Removing the Helmet, Part Two

From his position at the end of Part Two, Y attempts to escape the force of the leverage by softening his body. X quickly reaches up with his left hand and grabs Y's right wrist. X continues to turn forcefully to his right until he and Y are back to back. X holds on to Y's wrist tightly with his hands and does not allow the slightest gap between his head and Y's hand. X now lowers his head and bends forward from the waist while simultaneously lifting his arms upward. The left hand helps the right hand pull Y's arm downward. If the bending and pulling are done quickly, Y's arm will certainly be broken. See Figure 1-6c.

Figure 1-6c: Removing the Helmet, Part Three

Number Seven: Catching the Rat

This technique can be applied when an opponent leaps straight toward you, when he grabs or strikes you from the front, or when he grabs the front of your belt.

Explanation

Y charges X and strikes or grabs X's waist with one or both hands. X quickly parries Y's hands, pushing them outward to the sides, and then pulls him in, causing Y's body to lean forward, which prevents him from following up with a head butt attack. X brings both hands up and strikes the sides of Y's cheeks while hooking his fingers around the hinges of Y's jaw. X pulls on Y's jaw while he moves his lower body back. Y's whole body will be frozen on the spot and he will be unable to move his hands or feet.

Figure 1-7: Catching the Rat

Number Eight: Pressing the Head to Break the Neck

This technique is applied when the opponent strikes or charges in from the front.

Explanation

Y throws a straight right punch. X moves his body to the right and uses his right hand to quickly parry the force of Y's forward attack to the left. X simultaneously moves in to press his left chest area against Y's right ribs. X uses his right hand to push up and in below Y's chin. X reaches up behind Y's back with his left hand, his left elbow pushing into Y's back to keep Y from falling backward.

X extends his left hand over Y's head and then hooks his index and ring fingers into Y's eye sockets. X now pulls back and down forcefully with his left hand, causing Y to bend backward at the waist with his head tilted backward. X continues to use the coordinated power of both hands to pull Y's head to the rear with sudden force. Y's neck will be broken. If Y throws himself backward onto the ground to escape the technique, X can follow up with the Breaking the Waist technique (see Section Five). No matter what an opponent does to escape a technique, you should immediately follow up with another technique and maintain control. Unless you practice the techniques until they flow as naturally as water, you will not be able to beat others.

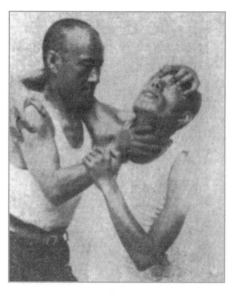

Figure 1-8: Pressing the Head to Break the Neck

Number Nine: Pressing the Sky Drum

This technique is useful when you encounter a strong opponent. Take advantage of the element of surprise and circle behind him to apply the technique.

Explanation

X comes upon Y while he is walking or sitting idly. X takes advantage of Y's lack of awareness and approaches from the rear. X thrusts his hands forward and upward from below Y's armpits, bringing his hands all the way up to the back of Y's neck. X pushes on Y's *tian gu* (sky drum) point, grabbing one of his wrists with the other hand. X presses forcefully forward and downward while lifting his arms upward; he leans his body back while pressing his stomach forward. Pressing with sudden force will cause unbearable pain in Y's neck. Y will feel dizzy and unable to resist and will be under X's control. If your opponent tries to fall on the ground and roll to escape the hold, it is important not to loosen your grip; instead, follow your opponent to the ground and continue applying pressure. The pressure will cause cervical dislocation and the opponent will be unable to escape.

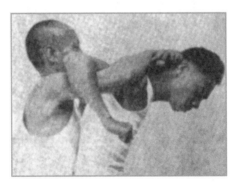

Figure 1-9: Pressing the Sky Drum

Section 2

Neck Techniques

Number One: Squeezing the Throat

This technique is applied when an opponent strikes toward your face or tries to grab your head.

Explanation

Y steps forward with his right foot and attacks with a straight right punch. X uses his right hand to parry Y's blow to the left. At the same time, X moves his body forward and presses his left shoulder into Y's right armpit. As X deflects Y's punch over the top of his left shoulder, he reaches his left hand up behind Y's back and grabs the top of Y's left shoulder. X forcefully pulls Y's shoulder inward, which prevents Y from using his left hand to attack. X now uses his thumb and index finger to forcefully squeeze Y's windpipe while pressing up into his Adam's apple, thereby closing off Y's air passage.

Figure 2-1: Squeezing the Throat

Number Two: Pinching with the Arm from the Front

This technique is applied when an opponent attempts to head butt your chest, or bends at the waist to attack your lower body.

Explanation

As Y rushes forward to head butt X's chest, X opens his arms and quickly dodges to his left while sucking in his stomach. Y will strike only air. X takes advantage of his position and takes a large step toward Y while bending forward at the waist and wrapping his right arm around the back of Y's neck. X pinches Y's neck tightly, squeezing the left carotid artery with his right upper arm as his right hand blocks off the right carotid artery. X reinforces the pressure by grabbing his right wrist with his left hand and pulling to increase the pressure on Y's neck. At the same time, X pulls upward

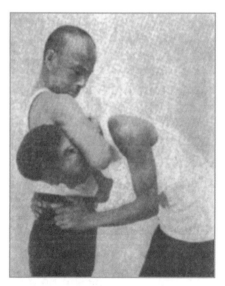

Figure 2-2: Pinching with the Arm from the Front

and lifts his chest while leaning back to further close off the flow of blood through Y's carotid arteries. Within three seconds Y will begin to lose consciousness; death will soon follow if the lock is not released. In this case, without proper resuscitation, Y will not survive. Therefore, this technique must not be used without just cause. If an opponent puts up a very strong defense, it is important not to let go of the hold. Fall down onto your back and lock your legs around the opponent's waist. Clamp down with your legs as you arch your back and your opponent will have no recourse and will stop resisting.

Number Three: Pinching with the Arm from the Rear

This technique can be applied when apprehending a suspect from behind or when engaged in hand-to-hand combat. It can be used to incapacitate or, if need be, kill your opponent.

Explanation

X comes upon Y, who is unaware of X's approach. X takes advantage of the situation and leaps behind Y, wrapping his left arm around Y's neck. X simultaneously extends his right arm and grabs the top of his right upper arm with his left hand. X bends his right arm and places his right palm on the back of Y's head. X presses forward with his right hand as he squeezes and pulls back with his left arm, blocking the flow of blood through Y's carotid arteries. Within three seconds, Y will lose consciousness, and without proper resuscitation, Y might die. This technique should not be used without just cause. During practice, if your partner starts to gag, you must immediately release the hold, or the risk of injury is great. This technique is also useful during hand-to-hand combat.

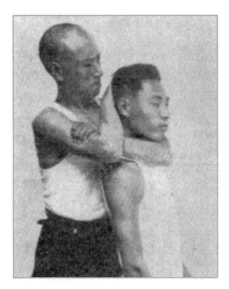

Figure 2-3: Pinching with the Arm from the Rear

Number Four: Front Throat Lock

This technique can be applied when an opponent has already been taken down to the ground, or when he or she is sitting or lying down.

Explanation

In this scenario, Y has already been taken down during hand-to-hand combat. X takes advantage of the situation and jumps on top of Y, pinching Y's waist between his legs. At the same time, X snakes his right hand inside to the right side of Y's collar and grabs the cloth; the back of his hand presses tightly against the back of Y's carotid artery. X does the same with his left hand on the left side of Y's neck. X holds the cloth of Y's collar firmly, with his wrists crossed in an "x." X then pulls forcefully to the left and right while twisting his hands upward so that his wrist bones (on the radial side of the wrists) press against Y's carotid arteries. Using much force, X pulls outward and toward himself. Within three seconds, the flow of blood will stop and Y will be rendered unconscious. Without proper resuscitation Y will not survive. This technique must only be used with just cause.

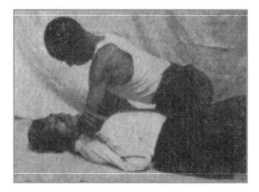

Figure 2-4: Front Throat Lock

Number Five: Rear Throat Lock

This technique can be applied during hand-to-hand combat or when an opponent is caught unaware.

Explanation

X finds Y sitting on the ground, unaware of X's approach. X takes advantage of the situation and begins his attack by circling to Y's right side. X snakes his left hand (palm facing forward) across the front of Y's throat, grabbing the left side of Y's collar. X then reaches below his own left hand to grab the cloth over Y's left shoulder with his right hand, with his palm facing downward. X's hands are now crossed at the wrists. X takes one step to his left and ends up standing behind Y. X pulls outward to the left and right as he pushes inward with his chest. This causes the left side of Y's collar to shut off the blood supply flowing through his left carotid artery. X's left wrist cuts off the flow of blood through Y's right carotid artery. Y will lose all power of resistance. Without proper resuscitation, Y will not recover. This technique must only be used with just cause. Those with lung problems should not allow others to practice this technique on them.

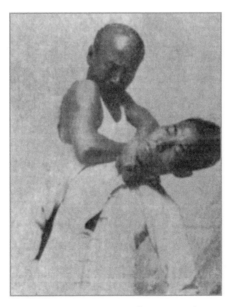

Figure 2-5:Rear Throat Lock

Number Six: Hand Block Throat Sealing

This technique can be used when apprehending a suspect, especially when you fear the suspect may call out for assistance. Application of this technique will cause the suspect to lose consciousness; he may be revived later when safely in custody. If the suspect does not come around on his own, it is important not to allow him to remain unconscious for more than two hours.

Explanation

X grabs the left side of Y's collar with his right hand in a palm-down grip. At the same time, X circles behind Y and raises his left arm up under Y's left armpit and places his arm behind Y's neck. X pulls up with force, causing Y's left arm to raise up next to X's

Figure 2-6: Hand Block Throat Sealing

left shoulder. At the same time, X pulls back with his right hand, causing Y's collar to cut off the flow of blood through his left carotid artery. X pushes down and forward with his left hand behind Y's neck so that the outside of his left palm cuts off the flow of blood through Y's right carotid artery. Within three seconds, the lack of blood flow will cause Y to lose consciousness. Without proper resuscitation, Y will not recover. This technique must not be applied without just cause.

Number Seven: Strangling the Neck and Breaking the Arm

This technique is applied during hand-to-hand combat. If you want to kill your opponent, you may strangle his neck. If you wish to simply break the opponent's arm, you can snap his elbow.

Explanation

X and Y are engaged in hand-to-hand mortal combat. X sees that Y has fallen to the ground. X quickly leaps onto Y and presses the back of Y's head with his chest. X inserts his right hand below Y's right armpit and reaches across to the left, encircling Y's arm. X grabs the back of Y's left collar with a palm-down grip and pulls back forcefully to choke him. At the same time, X moves his body upward, arches his head back, and stretches his legs forward. X pushes downward with his right shoulder as he pulls upward with his right elbow. At this point Y will be find it impossible to move or turn. If Y attempts to turn to his right, the choke becomes tighter and it will render him unconscious. If Y attempts to turn to his left, his elbow will be broken. If X chooses to continue applying force, he may break Y's arm and render him unconscious.

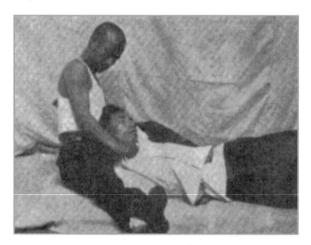

Figure 2-7: Hand Block Throat Sealing

Number Eight: Crossing the Neck

This technique is applied during hand-to-hand combat when both fighters are on the ground, or when an opponent is sitting or lying down. This technique will cause your opponent to lose consciousness.

Explanation

Y is on the ground. X uses the "Duck Floats on Water" form to leap onto Y's left side near his ribcage.

X wraps his left arm around Y's neck so that his upper arm is below Y's chin and his lower arm curls around the back of Y's neck. At the same time, X uses his right hand to push Y's left arm up and across to X's left shoulder. X drives his head downward; his left arm goes behind the lower part of Y's head as he presses his left shoulder in tightly. X grabs his left wrist with his right hand and pulls both hands forcefully toward his chest. X has his left leg bent beneath him and his right leg extended out to the side. X squeezes and drives in, pushing with his right foot. The tip of Y's left shoulder cuts off the flow of blood through his left carotid artery, while the lower part of X's arm cuts off the flow of blood through Y's right carotid artery. Within three seconds, Y will be unconscious. Without proper resuscitation, Y will not recover.

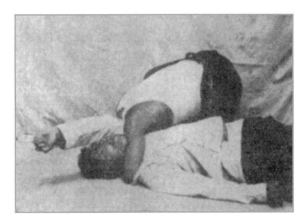

Figure 2-8: Crossing the Neck

Section **3**

Shoulder Techniques

Number One: Tread on the Arm Shoulder Lock

This technique is effective when dealing with a suspect who resists arrest.

Explanation

X comes across Y, who is walking. When Y's left arm is hanging down, X grabs Y's left hand with his left hand in a reverse grip. X presses the back of Y's hand with his thumb while his four fingers hook around the edge of Y's palm (on the ulna side) and press into the center of his hand. X forcefully grabs and pulls Y's hand upward and to the left while turning Y's fingers upward. X then grabs Y's hand with his right hand using the same reverse grip. X pushes against the back of Y's hand with both thumbs while twisting Y's hand toward his back. X continues to apply pressure forward and downward, causing Y's wrist to bend so that his fingers point upward.

Figure 3-1: Tread on the Arm Shoulder Lock

X pulls Y's hand toward his chest and then presses Y forward and down toward the ground. The pressure causes Y to fall down onto his knees. X pushes down forcefully on the back of Y's left shoulder with his right foot, causing Y to lie flat on the ground face down. X pushes Y's left hand up behind his left shoulder and then moves his right foot to press on the back of Y's upper arm.

X uses the front of his right shin to press forward against Y's lower arm. X's right foot presses downward forcefully while he drives his shin forward. Y is pinned to the ground unable to move. X has his hands free to tie up the opponent. If X has no rope, he can use his belt to secure Y's hands. If need be, X can quickly and forcefully press forward with his right shin to break Y's shoulder.

Number Two: Hooking the Elbow

This technique is applied when an opponent grabs the top of your lapel.

Explanation

Y grabs the top of X's right lapel with his left hand. X crosses his fingers and presses his hands into the back of Y's left elbow. X pulls inward as he presses downward. The pressure prevents Y from turning or escaping. At the same time, X turns his toes outward and presses the bottom of his right foot against the front of Y's left hip. X coordinates the pulling power of his hands with the pushing force of his foot to break Y's elbow.

Figure 3-2: Hooking the Elbow

Number Three: Grasping the Shoulder

This technique is used to control an opponent who grabs your shoulder.

Explanation

Y grabs X's right shoulder with his left hand while standing with either his right or left foot forward. With his left hand, X quickly presses the back of Y's hand tightly to his shoulder; while doing so, X steps back, pulling Y toward him. The backward movement extends Y's left arm until it is straight. X then presses forward with his right shoulder, causing Y's left wrist to bend backward. (First pull your opponent's arm straight, then push in to bend his wrist.) See Figure 3-3a.

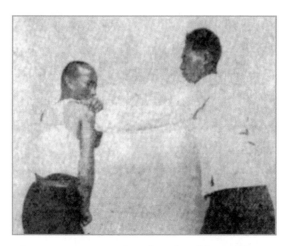

Figure 3-3a: Grasping the Shoulder, Part One

X continues the technique by lifting his right arm up and over the top of Y's left arm, circling it from right to left. As X circles his arm over Y's arm, he presses downward and turns his body to the left while maintaining strong pressure against the back of Y's left palm with his left hand. It is important for X to keep Y's left hand pinned tightly against his shoulder, as this will cause great pain in Y's wrist. X presses downward with his right arm as he bends his knees and squats. Y will not be able to resist the pressure. If X applies force, pressing downward with a sudden motion, Y's wrist will certainly be broken.

Figure 3-3b: Grasping the Shoulder, Part Two

Number Four: Hugging the Elbow

This technique is applied when an opponent slips out of the Grasping the Shoulder technique.

Explanation

X applies the previous technique, Grasping the Shoulder. Y contracts his arm and uses the Method of Softness to escape the hold. X follows up by using the Method of Sticking and Following and prevents Y from escaping by stepping forward with his right foot and wrapping his right arm upward from below Y's left arm past Y's back and around Y's shoulder. At the same time, X places his left arm on the back of Y's upper arm. X presses downward forcefully with both arms, causing Y to bend forward at the waist. X pulls his right arm back so that his forearm presses on the back of Y's elbow. X then grabs his right wrist with his left hand. X forcefully pulls his right arm in toward his chest, hugging Y's arm tightly as he straightens his torso. Y's arm will be broken. (Note that in Figure 3-4, the technique is being done on the opposite side as the description.)

Figure 3-4: Hugging the Elbow

Number Five: Blocking the Wing

Blocking the Wing is an alternative follow up technique for when an opponent attempts to escape from Grasping the Shoulder.

Explanation

Y grabs X's left shoulder with his right hand. X applies the Grasping the Shoulder technique, but Y attempts to escape by pulling his right arm free of the hold. X maintains contact with his left hand and uses the Method of Sticking and Following to adhere to Y's arm. X sticks to Y's arm and moves in while inserting his left arm below Y's right shoulder and raising his arm. At the same time, X moves his right hand past the right side of Y's face and presses downward on the back of Y's neck with the edge of his hand. X places his left hand over his right and comes into position with his hands crossed and Y's right arm trapped over X's left shoulder. See Figure 3-5a.

Figure 3-5a: Blocking the Wing, Part One

X continues the move by pushing downward as he pulls inward with both arms. X simultaneously pushes upward and forward with his left shoulder as he bends forward from the waist while moving his hips backward. This prevents Y from rolling out of the hold. If X applies force suddenly, he will dislocate Y's shoulder.

If Y is very flexible, the hold may have little effect. In this case, X bends forward even further and grabs Y's left wrist with both hands. X forcefully pulls Y's wrist back toward his chest and presses outward with his shoulder. Y's right shoulder will definitely be dislocated. If X continues to pull Y's left arm inward and upward, he will also dislocate Y's left shoulder. See Figure 3-5b.

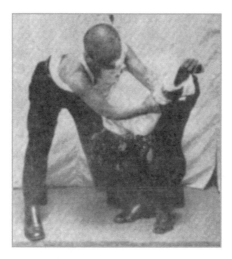

Figure 3-5b: Blocking the Wing, Part Two

Number Six: Pinching the Arm Shoulder Dislocation

This technique is used to capture an enemy who is sitting or lying on the ground.

Explanation

If Y is sitting or lying down, X leaps forward and straddles Y's chest. X's pinches his knees against the sides of Y's chest, preventing Y from turning over. Y must now strike upward in an attempt to escape. X takes advantage of Y's striking and crossing his arms, he presses Y's hands forcefully to the ground, pinning them above Y's head. At the same time, X pivots his body and kneels above Y's head, while pulling Y's arms up and together. X then pinches Y's arms between his knees. The pinch will dislocate Y's shoulders. Because the application of this technique involves changing the position of the hands and knees, it is difficult for beginners to execute it successfully. This technique must be practiced until it is second nature in order to be applied in combat.

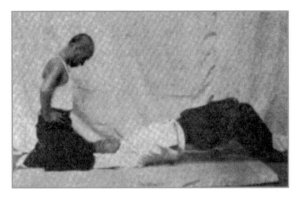

Figure 3-6: Pinching the Arm Shoulder Dislocation

Section **4**

Chest, Ribs, and Back Techniques

Number One: Rear Elbow Lifting

This technique is applied when an opponent grabs the back of your collar.

Explanation

In this scenario, X is walking along when Y grabs his collar from behind. X does not need to turn around; instead, he reaches back with his right hand and grabs the back of Y's right hand. X presses Y's hand tightly to the back of his neck and leans forward while stepping forward with his right foot, pulling Y's right arm straight. See Figure 4-1a.

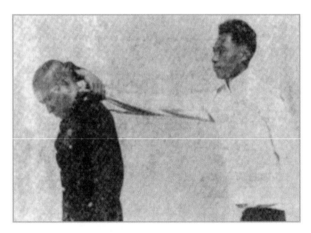

Figure 4-1a: Rear Elbow Lifting, Part One

Now that X has trapped Y's right hand, he quickly turns to his left, turning parallel to Y. At the same time, X bends his left arm and pushes upward at just below the point of Y's elbow. X pushes up suddenly and forcefully with his left hand as he leans his head back and pulls downward with his right hand. If this move is done quickly and forcefully, it will certainly break Y's elbow. See Figure 4-1b.

Figure 4-1b: Rear Elbow Lifting, Part Two

Number Two: Moving the Elbow

This technique is also applied when an opponent grabs the back of your collar.

Explanation

Y grabs the back of X's collar. X quickly reaches back with his right hand and tightly grabs the back of Y's hand. X takes a step back with his right foot as he simultaneously bends his left arm and wraps it around the back of Y's elbow. X pushes Y's elbow horizontally. X's right hand must hold onto Y's hand tightly as he twists Y's right hand upward. X must be careful to prevent Y from twisting his arm downward to escape the hold. X then lifts his left leg and stretches it across the front of Y's hips or legs; he presses his leg back into Y forcefully to block Y's forward movement. X then bends forward as he twists his body back toward the right. Pressure should be applied suddenly, with force, and in a snapping motion (as if releasing a bow); if you apply the pressure slowly, the lock will not work.

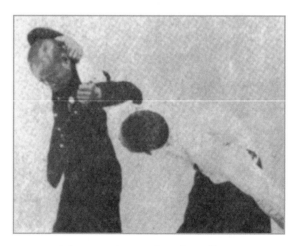

Figure 4-2: Moving the Elbow

Number Three: Turn the Body and Break the Wrist

This technique is applied when an opponent grabs your lapels.

Explanation

Y steps up with his left foot forward and grabs X's lapels with his right hand. X grabs the back of Y's right hand with his right hand and wraps his middle finger around the outer edge of Y's hand so that the finger presses tightly against the inside of Y's palm. At the same time, X strikes the crook of Y's elbow with a forceful downward motion of his left forearm, causing Y's arm to bend at the elbow. X presses Y's right arm tightly against his ribs, which prevents Y from straightening the arm. X then turns his torso to his right while pressing forward with his chest. This motion will break Y's wrist.

Figure 4-3: Turn the Body and Break the Wrist

Number Four: Lying Hoof

This technique is also applied when an opponent grabs your lapels.

Explanation

Y grabs X's lapels with his right hand. X quickly grabs the back of Y's hand with his right hand and wraps his middle finger around the outer edge of Y's hand so that his middle finger presses tightly against the inside of Y's palm. X presses Y's hand firmly against his body. X pulls Y's hand backward and simultaneously grabs Y's wrist from below with his left hand. X keeps his elbows pressed tightly to his sides in preparation for the second part of the technique. See Figure 4-4a.

Figure 4-4a: Lying Hoof, Part One

To continue the move, X presses his upper body against Y's hand and then pulls back forcefully. (By first pressing forward and then pulling backward, X negates Y's resistance.) At the same time, X uses the outside edge of his left palm to press up into Y's wrist, causing the wrist to bend downward. X now turns his body slightly to the right while continuing to press his body against Y's hand in a downward direction. It is important for X to keep his elbows squeezed tightly against the sides of his body. The entire weight of X's body is suddenly and quickly pressed into Y's hand, causing Y's body to bend forward as he drops down onto his left hand for support. See Figure 4-4b.

Figure 4-4b: Lying Hoof, Part Two

Number Five: Pressing the Elbow

This is third alternative for when an opponent grabs your lapels.

Explanation

Y grabs X's lapels with his right hand. X quickly grabs the back of Y's hand with his right hand. X thrusts his chest forward to stop Y's attacking force and then pulls forcefully backward and to the right. At the same time, X uses his left forearm to press on the back of Y's elbow with a sudden pulse of force. As he presses, X turns his body to the right and drops his weight forward. If Y is able to withstand the pressure, X can follow up with the Moving the Elbow technique by lifting his left leg and pressing the back of his leg against Y's hips or legs. X then snaps his leg back into Y as he puts pressure against Y's elbow, which will certainly be injured.

Figure 4-5: Pressing the Elbow

Number Six: Forcing the Wrist

This technique is applied when an opponent reaches forward to grab your chest.

Explanation

With his right hand, Y grabs X's chest near his left armpit. Before Y has the chance to completely close his grip, X grabs the back of Y's upper arm with his left hand, placing his hand behind Y's elbow. At the same time, X uses the outer edge of his right palm to chop forcefully at the back of Y's wrist, which causes Y's wrist to bend upward. X then grabs behind Y's elbow with his right hand and simultaneously pushes forward with the left side of his chest as he pulls inward forcefully with his hands. X leans his body forward as he thrusts his chest out in a quick and forceful motion. The pressure bends Y's wrist back.

Figure 4-6: Forcing the Wrist

Number Seven: Receiving the Wrist

This technique is applied as an opponent reaches forward to grab your chest.

Explanation

Y reaches forward with his right hand, palm facing downward, to grab X's chest. Y may have either foot forward. Before Y is able to grab him, X moves his chest back and grabs Y's upper arm just above the elbow with his left hand. At the same time, X closes the fingers of his right hand together and using the radial side of his palm, strikes upward into Y's wrist. Y's wrist will bend upward and the back of his hand will be pressed against X's chest. X then reinforces his grip on Y's upper arm by moving his right hand to Y's arm. Finally, X suddenly pulls in as he pushes his chest forward. This prevents Y from straightening his wrist or moving it left or right.

Figure 4-7: Receiving the Wrist

Number Eight: Reverse Elbow Lifting

This technique is applied when an opponent grabs your chest just below your throat.

Explanation

With his right hand, Y grabs X's chest just below X's throat. Y may be standing with either foot forward. X quickly grabs Y's hand with his right hand. At the same time, X strikes Y's forearm with his left hand, which causes Y's arm to bend. As he strikes, X turns his upper body and leans forward while pulling his stomach in. X's left hand now pushes Y's elbow from below—first toward the front and to the right and then upward. As he pushes upward, X leans his upper body back slightly. A sudden push will break Y's elbow.

Figure 4-8: Reverse Elbow Lifting

Section **5**

Waist and Stomach Techniques

Number One: Forward Springing Elbow

This technique is applied when an opponent grabs the clothing around your waist.

Explanation

With his left hand, Y grabs X's waist or belt with a palm-down grip. X grabs Y's hand tightly with his left hand and prevents Y from pulling his hand away. X then takes a big step with his right leg, putting his foot down either behind or in front of Y's legs. X bends forward forcefully as he extends his right arm under Y's left armpit and across Y's chest and ribs. Twisting his right palm backward and downward, X forcefully snaps his right arm behind Y's elbow. As he applies sudden pressure behind Y's elbow, X simultaneously turns his body to his left. The arms and legs must move together quickly; it is very important not to move too slowly when applying this technique.

Figure 5-1: Forward Springing Elbow

Number Two: Rear Springing Elbow

This technique is applied when an opponent grabs your waist or belt from behind.

Explanation

While X is walking, Y attacks him by grabbing X's waist or belt from behind with his right hand. X quickly reaches back with his right hand and grabs Y's hand. X pulls forward forcefully as he takes a big step forward with his right foot. See Figure 5-2a. This sets up the second part of the technique.

Figure 5-2a: Rear Springing Elbow, Part One

X then extends his left arm back behind himself and keeping his fingers closed, he wraps his left arm around Y's right arm from above, passing it under Y's right armpit and across Y's chest. (The back of X's left hand is pressed into Y's chest.) At the same time, X steps his left foot across the front of Y's right leg, bends his body forward and twists his left palm downward. X uses the twisting force of his left arm to snap it forcefully behind Y's elbow. X simultaneously swings his head around to his right; his body and arm follow this movement to the right rear side in one forceful pulling motion. See Figure 5-2b.

Figure 5-2b: Rear Springing Elbow, Part Two

Number Three: Forcing the Wrist

This technique is applied when an opponent grabs your belt or the clothing at your stomach.

Explanation

Y tries to grab the front of X's belt with his right hand. X uses the power of his lower abdomen and thrusts his belly forward as he moves his body toward Y. X then pulls backward, at the same time grabbing the back of Y's upper arm with his left hand. X pushes forward again. Between the forward and backward movements, the force of Y's grip will be dispersed. X takes advantage of the situation and with his right palm, he chops down forcefully from above to the top of Y's wrist, causing Y's wrist to bend upward. See Figure 5-3a. Y is now set up for the second part of the technique.

Figure 5-3a: Forcing the Wrist, Part One

X has already bent Y's wrist. Now, X uses his right hand to reinforce his left grip—both hands grab the back of Y's right arm. X pulls Y inward forcefully with both hands as he simultaneously thrusts out his lower abdomen. X applies force suddenly, thereby preventing Y from pulling his arm free and causing great pain in Y's wrist. See Figure 5-3b.

Figure 5-3b: Forcing the Wrist, Part Two

Number Four: Lifting the Elbow

This technique is applied when an opponent grabs your belt with a palm-up grip.

Explanation

Y steps forward with his right foot and grabs X's belt with a palm-up grip. X leans his upper body forward and pulls his stomach in as he grabs Y's upper arm with both hands. X pulls forcefully upward and inward as he presses downward with his chest. X then turns out the toes of his left foot and presses the sole of his foot against the front of Y's right hip. X forcefully kicks forward and downward as he leans his upper body back and pulls Y's arm upward and inward. If X applies force suddenly, he will break Y's wrist.

Figure 5-4: Lifting the Elbow

Number Five: Pressing the Elbow

This is an alternative technique for when an opponent grabs your belt with a palm-up grip.

Explanation

Y grabs X's belt with a palm-up grip. X grabs Y's attacking hand tightly with his right hand, preventing Y from withdrawing his arm. X leans his upper body forward and pulls his stomach in while forcefully pulling Y's arm straight. At the same time, X wraps his left arm around Y's elbow from below, pressing upward forcefully at the point of Y's elbow. X presses downward with his right hand and leans his upper body back. Y cannot step out to escape and his elbow will be broken.

Figure 5-5: Pressing the Elbow

Number Six: Stopping the Wrist

This is yet another technique that can be applied when an opponent grabs your belt with a palm-up grip.

Explanation

With his right hand, Y grabs X's belt or waist with a palm-up grip. Before Y has fully secured his grip, X quickly grabs Y's elbow from below with his left hand and pulls inward. At the same time, X closes the fingers of his right hand and does an upward strike to the downward-facing side of Y's wrist using the inside edge of his palm as a striking surface. The strike causes Y's wrist to bend upward so that Y's palm is pressed tightly against X's stomach. X then grabs Y's upper arm with his right hand, placing it next to his left hand in order to reinforce his grip, and pulls inward forcefully while simultaneously thrusting his stomach outward. The opposing pressures of the hands pulling inward and the stomach thrusting outward will break Y's wrist.

Figure 5-6: Stopping the Wrist

Number Seven: Breaking the Waist

Practitioners should note that this technique is difficult to apply without the appropriate opportunity.

Explanation

Using a throwing method, X knocks Y to the ground toward X's left side. As Y falls, X squats and extends his left knee beneath Y's waist in the Qilin form. At the same time, X pushes down with both hands, his left hand on Y's chest and his right hand on Y's pubic bone. X pushes down with sudden force while simultaneously raising his left heel, causing Y's waist to fold.

Figure 5-7: Breaking the Waist

Number Eight: Pinching the Waist

This technique can pull victory from the jaws of defeat. If an opponent attacks ferociously, fall back onto the ground and apply this technique.

Explanation

Y attacks X ferociously. X is afraid he will not be able to move out of the way quickly enough, so he receives the attack by catching Y's hands and falling down onto his back. As he falls, X lifts his feet and wraps his legs around Y's waist, squeezing the sides of Y's ribs. X crosses his ankles and squeezes his knees together tightly in order to break Y's ribs and burst Y's diaphragm. If the defender has short legs or the opponent is very large, this technique will not be easy to apply. This technique must not be taken lightly: if the diaphragm bursts, there will be no hope of saving the opponent's life.

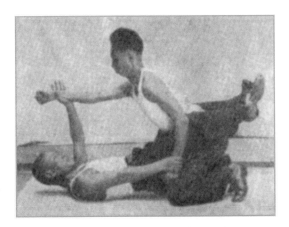

Figure 5-8: Pinching the Waist

Section **6**

Arm and Wrist Techniques

Number One: Small Entwining

This technique is applied when an opponent grabs your wrist.

Explanation

X extends his right hand to grab Y, but Y quickly seizes X's wrist. X immediately grabs the back of Y's hand tightly, with his thumb down and his four fingers on the top of the hand. This will prevent Y from withdrawing his hand. X then traps Y's hand between his hands and pushes forward, forcing Y to resist by pushing back. X takes advantage of Y's pushing motion to further pull Y's hand into him. Y will again be forced to resist and will pull away. X takes advantage of Y's pulling motion and moves his right hand up and over the top of Y's wrist, hooking the wrist tightly. Y is now set up for the second part of the technique. See Figure 6-1a.

Figure 6-1a: Small Entwining, Part One

X then closes the fingers of his right hand and grabs the top of Y's wrist with his four fingers as he hooks his thumb below Y's wrist. X pushes downward forcefully on the outside of Y's wrist. X's middle finger presses downward and to the left, preventing Y from bending or twisting his arm. The pressure on Y's wrist will force him to his knees, and he won't have the power to resist the technique. If need be, X can use sudden force, pulling backward and downward to break Y's wrist.

Figure 6-1b: Small Entwining, Part Two

Number Two: Double Entwining

This technique is used specifically to counter the Small Entwining technique.

Explanation

Y captures X with the Small Entwining technique. Before Y has applied full force, X quickly relaxes his right hand and lifts his right elbow. X reaches up between Y's chest and hands with his left hand (his palm faces inward). X raises his arm up from below his captured right hand (and Y's hands) to relieve the pressure on his wrist. X is now ready for the second part of the technique. See Figure 6-2a.

Figure 6-2a: Double Entwining, Part One

X pulls down with his left hand, grabbing Y's middle finger (or all of his fingers). X pulls Y's hand downward and inward, hugging Y's hand forcefully to his chest. At the same time, X raises his right elbow over the top of Y's left wrist and presses down on Y's arm. X keeps Y's hand stuck tightly to his chest as he applies the downward pressure. X lifts his heels and comes up on the balls of his feet while leaning his body forward. X then drops his heels as he presses down forcefully with both hands. The pressure will force Y to his knees. At this point, X can release his right hand and control Y only with his left hand. See Figure 6-2b.

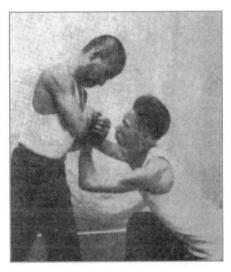

Figure 6-2b: Double Entwining, Part Two

Number Three: Big Entwining

This technique is applied when you encounter an opponent who is so strong the Small Entwining technique is ineffective against him.

Explanation

X reaches forward with his right hand to grab Y. Y steps up with his right foot and grabs X's wrist with his right hand. X takes advantage of the situation and pulls his right hand back to his chest as he steps his left foot behind Y's right leg. At the same time, X reaches up from under Y's right arm with his left hand and grabs the back of Y's right wrist. X is now set up for the next part of the technique. See Figure 6-3a.

Figure 6-3a: Big Entwining, Part One

X presses downward with his left hand as he twists outward and to the right. X forcefully pulls both hands back toward his chest while gripping Y tightly. X is now ready for the third part of the technique. See Figure 6-3b.

Figure 6-3b: Big Entwining, Part Two

To complete the sequence, X uses a twisting force to cut downward and inward with his right hand while turning the hand outward. X's fingers grip downward with twisting force as his lower left arm pulls in horizontally toward his chest. X's upper body follows the motion—he leans forward and then twists back and to the left. The pressure generated by this movement will force Y to his knees. Y's wrist will be broken, and he will be powerless to resist capture. See Figure 6-3c.

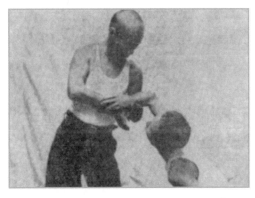

Figure 6-3c: Big Entwining, Part Three

Number Four: Bend the Elbow and Break the Arm

This technique is applied when an opponent attacks you with the Pressing the Top of Tai Mountain technique.

Explanation

Y uses his right fist to strike downward with the Pressing the Top of Tai Mountain technique or to attack straight to the face. X blocks the strike with his lower arm; his left foot is forward. See Figure 6-4a.

Figure 6-4a: Bend the Elbow and Break the Arm, Part One

After blocking the strike, X steps forward with his right foot and reaching up from below, he hooks his right hand forcefully over the top of Y's forearm. At the same time, X pulls outward forcefully with his left lower arm as he grabs Y's wrist with his left hand. X hooks and pulls Y's arm until it is bent and Y is unable to free his arm. See Figure 6-4b.

Y will certainly attempt to escape from the hold or he will try another attack. Whether Y moves forward or backward, X must react as quick as lightning and use his right hand to grip the back of Y's hand, with his middle, ring, and little fingers hooking over the outer edge of Y's palm. X then pulls down forcefully with his hands as he lifts his right elbow upward. This move might break or dislocate Y's elbow, but even if it doesn't do either, the pain in Y's elbow will prevent him from resisting capture. See Figure 6-4c.

Figure 6-4b: Bend the Elbow and Break the Arm, Part Two

Figure 6-4c: Bend the Elbow and Break the Arm, Part Three

Number Five: Holding a Basket

This technique is applied when an opponent attempts to grab your chest. It is always useful for apprehending a criminal—you can capture him by controlling his hand.

Explanation

Y extends his right hand to grab X in the center of his chest. Before Y completes his attack, X grabs Y's hand from below with his left hand using a palm-to-palm grip. At the same time, X opens his right thumb outward and closes his four fingers together so that they form a slight curve. X then strikes the crook of Y's elbow horizontally, making contact with the fleshy part between his thumb and forefinger. Y is now set up for the second part of the technique. See Figure 6-5a.

Figure 6-5a: Holding a Basket, Part One

The strike to the crook of Y's elbow will cause his elbow to bend. X then bends his left elbow and uses his right hand to push Y's right elbow down and to the left into X's left armpit. X pinches

Y's arm forcefully with his left arm, squeezing it against his chest. This will cause Y's wrist to bend as well. With his left hand, X twists Y's hand downward and inward. If X uses sufficient force, Y will be held captive with no chance of resisting.

Figure 6-5b: Holding a Basket, Part Two

If an opponent is exceptionally strong or has an very flexible wrist, X will need to squeeze Y's arm tightly with his left arm and then move his right hand to grip Y's right hand, with his thumb hooked around the outer edge of Y's palm and his four fingers gripping the back of Y's hand. X twists outward forcefully with his right hand as his left hand pulls Y inward. Y will unable to resist the hold, and X can lead his opponent away. If an opponent refuses to walk, X can increase the pressure on his wrist, causing him unbearable pain and forcing him to comply. If X applies force suddenly, Y's wrist will be broken.

Number Six: Binding the Tiger

This technique is applied when apprehending a criminal. Take advantage of the situation to seize and then control the opponent.

Explanation

X walks up to Y from the front and plans to capture him. X moves slightly to his left and then suddenly extends his right hand with the palm down and grabs the back of Y's right hand. X's thumb presses the back of Y's hand and his four fingers fold around the outside of Y's hand with the fingertips pressed tightly against the inside of Y's palm. See Figure 6-6a.

Figure 6-6a: Binding the Tiger, Part One

X then raises his right up and to his right, turning Y's hand over. X reinforces his hold with his left hand, also pressing his left thumb into the back of Y's hand with his four fingers folding around the inside of Y's hand. X presses forcefully against the back of Y's hand with his thumbs while he pulls back and down with his fingers hooked around Y's wrist. X moves his lower body back as he presses downward and pulls inward with his arms. The force will cause Y to bend forward at the waist and go down onto his hand and knees. See Figure 6-6b.

Figure 6-6b: Binding the Tiger, Part Two

As Y starts to fall, X pushes forward and downward while continuing to cut downward into Y's wrist. At the same time, X takes a big step forward with his left foot, placing the foot beside Y's hip. X shifts his weight to his left leg—the pressure will force Y's right shoulder and face into the ground. Y's left arm will be on the ground, unable to move. X twists Y's right arm up and bends Y's elbow as he bends forward to press his weight into Y's wrist. X presses his left knee against the outside of Y's right hip to prevent Y from rolling out of the hold. Y is now pinned on the ground. See Figure 6-6c.

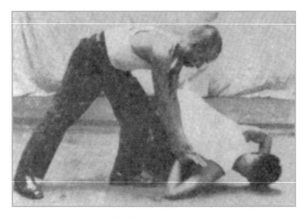

Figure 6-6c: Binding the Tiger, Part Three

With Y on the ground, X turns left and continues to press his left knee to Y's hip as he steps his right foot up and onto the back of Y's upper arm. X presses down forcefully with his right leg until Y's forearm is forced above his shoulder. X then releases his grips and pushes Y's arm to the left until X's knee pins Y's upper arm against his lower back. X presses forcefully forward with both legs, pinning Y so that he cannot move his arms or legs. X's hands are now free to bind Y's hands. If X doesn't have a rope or handcuffs, he may use his belt to tie up Y. If need be, X can push his right foot up and to the left with force, which will dislocate Y's shoulder and elbow. See Figure 6-6d.

Figure 6-6d: Binding the Tiger, Part Four

Number Seven: Rolling the Elbow

This technique is applied when an opponent attacks with a straight punch.

Explanation

Y steps forward with his right foot and throws a right straight punch at X's chest or face. X moves his chest back and turns a little to his right, slipping away from Y's punch. At the same time, X grabs Y's fist with both hands—left hand on the top and right hand on the bottom. X hooks his thumbs around the back of Y's fist and hooks his fingers around the inside of Y's hand. X pulls forcefully to his right; Y will react by pulling back strongly. See Figure 6-7a.

Figure 6-7a: Rolling Elbow, Part One

X takes advantage of Y's force and relaxing his own force, he follows Y's pull while taking a large step forward with his right foot, placing it behind Y's right leg. At the same time, X moves his right elbow over Y's arm and pinches Y's arm between his arm and chest. X twists Y's wrist downward and outward, forcing Y to bend his arm. X leans forward with his upper body and while turning his head back to the left, he falls to the ground. Y will be unable to resist. See Figure 6-7b.

Figure 6-7b: Rolling Elbow, Part Two

As Y is lying on his back, X takes advantage of the falling momentum and pushes off strongly with both feet, rolling forward over his right shoulder. If the timing of the roll is precise, Y's elbow will certainly be broken. This part of the technique must not be done forcefully in practice. If you wish to train this move for greater agility, you should let go of your opponent's arm before doing the roll. Practicing this technique while maintaining your grip on your opponent's arm is very dangerous. See Figure 6-7c.

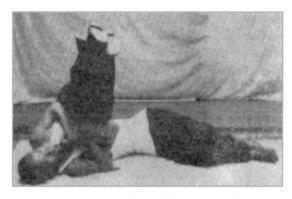

Figure 6-7c: Rolling Elbow, Part Three

Number Eight: Pulling the Wing

This technique is applied when an opponent reaches for the center of your chest.

Explanation

Y reaches forward with his right hand to grab X's chest. X takes advantage of Y's motion and before Y has a chance to complete his move, X grabs Y's hand with his left hand and hits Y's wrist, striking upward with his right hand. X then pushes forward with his left hand as his right hand hooks around Y's hand forcefully, causing Y's wrist to bend upward. See Figure 6-8a. For the technique to be successful, you must quickly follow up this initial sequence with the next move.

Figure 6-8a: Pulling the Wing, Part One

X quickly twists Y's hand downward and outward with his left hand while his right hand grabs Y's other hand. X's thumb presses the back of Y's hand as his fingers wrap around the outside of Y's palm. X moves his body backward and uses both hands to pull Y's hand downward. Y will twist and bend forward as his elbow bends. If X continues to apply force, he will break Y's arm. See Figure 6-8b.

Figure 6-8b: Pulling the Wing, Part Two

Number Nine: Tearing the Wing

This technique is used to control an opponent who approaches you head on.

Explanation

X approaches Y and plans to take him into custody. X moves to his left and as he passes Y, he grabs the back of Y's hand at the wrist with his right hand. X presses his thumb into the back of Y's hand and wraps his fingers around Y's hand so that his fingertips press into Y's palm. X grabs Y's hand tightly in preparation for the second part of the technique. See Figure 6-9a.

Figure 6-9a: Tearing the Wing, Part One

X then lifts Y's hand and twists it to the right. X presses his thumb into Y's hand with force as his four fingers hook and pull tightly around the outer edge of Y's palm. Y's hand will bend upward from the wrist. At the same time, X reinforces his grip with his left hand—his left thumb also presses the back of Y's hand as his four fingers hook around into Y's palm. X moves his body backward and pulls Y's arm while forcefully twisting it to the right with both hands. The leverage will cause Y to bend forward at the waist. The pain in his wrist will prevent Y from resisting. If X applies sudden force, he will break Y's wrist. See Figure 6-9b.

Figure 6-9b: Tearing the Wing, Part Two

Y attempts to escape by softening his body and turning to his left as he bends his elbow to relieve the pressure of the hold. X reacts quickly as Y turns, pushing Y's right arm forcefully up against his back. At the same time, X grabs the top of Y's right or left shoulder with his left hand and pushes downward. The opposing upward and downward forces of X's hands cause Y to turn his back to X. If X applies sudden force, it will break both Y's shoulder and his wrist. See Figure 6-9c.

Figure 6-9c: Tearing the Wing, Part Three

Number Ten: Resisting the Elbow

This technique is applied when an opponent attacks with a straight punch.

Explanation

Y attacks with a right straight punch to X's face. X moves to his left and captures Y's hand; he brings his right hand down on the punch from above (palm facing downward) as he brings his left hand up from below the punch (palm facing upward). As X grabs Y's wrist with both hands, he simultaneously pulls Y's arm toward himself and turns his body to the right rear. X brings Y's right elbow down on top of his left shoulder. X pulls downward with his hands and presses upward with his shoulder as he leans his body slightly forward. If the movements of X's shoulder and hands are coordinated and quick, Y's body will be extended and his heels will leave the ground, leaving him powerless to resist. The force may also break Y's elbow.

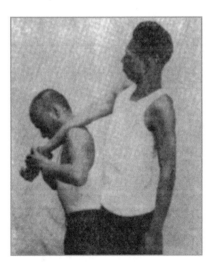

Figure 6-10: Resisting the Elbow

Number Eleven: Rolling the Fist

This technique is applied when an opponent throws an uppercut at your center or solar plexus.

Explanation

Y throws an uppercut at X's stomach. X dodges to his left and uses both hands to capture Y's incoming punch; his thumbs press the back of Y's hand and his fingers hook around to the inside of Y's wrist. X twists both of his hands to his left, bending Y's fist upward. At the same time, X hooks inward forcefully with his middle fingers, presses forward with his thumbs, and pulls Y's fist downward and back. While applying force, X also pushes his hips back. If X applies sudden force, Y will be forced to his knees as his wrist breaks.

Figure Resisting the Elbow

Number Twelve: Plucking the Wrist

This technique is applied after you seize the Ma Mu points. These points are located on the upper arm just above and to the side of the crook of the elbow. When your opponent attempts to escape the pain caused by your grip on these points, apply the technique.

Explanation

X grabs Y's left hand with his left hand. X hooks his thumb into the center of Y's palm as his fingers press on the back of Y's hand. X uses force and grabs Y's hand tightly. At the same time, X uses his thumb and middle finger to pinch Y's Ma Mu points. X squeezes the points forcefully from above and below and pulls Y's arm toward his chest. Y will feel soreness and weakness throughout his body. See Figure 6-12a.

Figure 6-12a: Plucking the Wrist, Part One

Y will try to escape the hold by pulling his arm back and lifting his elbow. X takes advantage of Y's force and pushes forward forcefully with his left hand as he plucks Y's hand inward, causing his wrist to bend. X simultaneously pushes outward with his right hand—all movements are done quickly. Y's wrist will be broken. See Figure 6-12b.

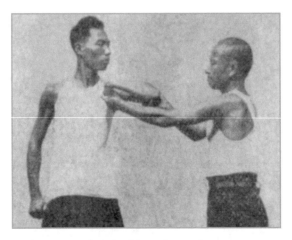

Figure 6-12b: Plucking the Wrist, Part Two

Number Thirteen: Pinching the Sleeve

This technique is applied when an opponent strikes toward your chest. You may also use it to seize him suddenly when he is not prepared for the attack.

Explanation

Y strikes toward X's chest with his left hand. X catches the blow with his left hand while his right hand circles over the top of Y's arm from above. X pinches Y's left upper arm tightly with his right arm. The radial side of X's right wrist forcefully presses up against Y's arm about two inches behind the point of Y's elbow. At the same time, X pushes Y's arm downward with his left hand. Y's elbow will be broken.

Figure 6-13: Pinching the Sleeve

Number Fourteen: Hooking the Fist

You can apply this technique when an opponent grabs your sleeve.

Explanation

Y grabs X's right sleeve with his left hand. X turns his right hand over and hooks the outside of Y's wrist with the fleshy part between his thumb and forefinger. X presses downward as he pulls Y's wrist backward. At the same time, X uses his left hand to press the back of Y's hand forward and upward as he turns his body to the left. X presses in strongly and suddenly to break Y's wrist.

Figure 6-14: Hooking the Fist

Number Fifteen: Supporting the Elbow and Breaking the Wrist

This technique is used to break an opponent's wrist during a furious fight when both fighters fall to the ground.

Explanation

Y falls to the ground. X takes advantage of the situation and follows him, lying down on the left side of Y's chest. X pinches Y's left arm between his legs so that Y's palm faces upward. X places his left thigh below Y's upper arm, and his right thigh presses downward on Y's lower arm from above. As X presses down on Y's right hand, bending Y's elbow, he threads his left hand under Y's armpit to grab Y's right wrist. X pulls Y's hand back as he lifts the arm, causing Y's wrist to break as he also breaks Y's left elbow with his legs.

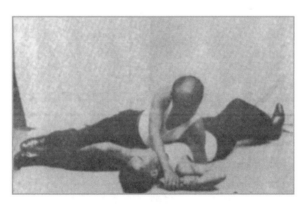

Figure 6-15: Supporting the Elbow and Breaking the Wrist

Number Sixteen: Blocking the Elbow

This technique is used to break an opponent's elbow during hand-to-hand combat when he has fallen or is already sitting on the ground.

Explanation

Y has fallen to the ground and starts to get up. X quickly grabs Y's left wrist with both hands while stepping his right leg over Y's head. X now snaps his left leg back forcefully while twisting Y's arm so that the back of Y's elbow is across X's left thigh. X pulls back with both hands as he pushes back with his right leg to break Y's elbow.

Figure 6-16: Blocking the Elbow

Number Seventeen: Lifting the Elbow

This technique is applied when an opponent grabs the bottom of your sleeve.

Explanation

Y grabs the bottom of X's right sleeve with his right hand. X grabs Y's right wrist from above with his right hand and forcefully pulls Y's hand back and to his right. At the same time, X bends his left elbow and strikes upward, hitting Y's elbow two inches below its point with the crook of his elbow. X then bends his left leg and forcefully presses his shin against Y's waist. X leans to his right and turns his head to the right as he pushes up with his left arm and pushes down with his right hand. Y's elbow will break.

Figure 6-17: Lifting the Elbow

Number Eighteen: Pressing the Elbow

When an opponent grabs your right hand with his right hand, you can apply the technique of Small Entwining (explained earlier in the chapter). If an opponent grabs your right hand with his left hand, apply this technique.

Explanation

Y grabs X's right hand with his left hand. X grabs Y's left hand with his left hand and pulls Y in toward his chest. X turns his body to the left and twists his right elbow over so that it presses down on the back of Y's left arm. X bends his body forward as he turns backward. Y's elbow will break.

Figure 6-18: Pressing the Elbow

Number Nineteen: Springing Elbow Press

This technique is applied when an opponent grabs the clothing around your waist.

Explanation

Y grabs X's clothing on the left side of his waist. X bends his upper body forward while forcefully pushing the crook of his left elbow upward from just below the point of Y's right elbow. At the same time, X pushes his right hand against Y's upper arm until he can grab his own right arm just above the elbow with his left hand. X snaps his left arm upward in a springlike motion as he pushes downward with his right palm. As he applies pressure, X also leans his body back. The opposing forces will break Y's elbow.

Figure 6-19: Springing Elbow Press

Number Twenty: Pinching the Elbow

This technique is applied to break an opponent's elbow and control him when he is already on the ground.

Explanation

Y is on the ground. X takes advantage of the situation and jumps on top of Y so that he is at a ninety-degree angle to Y's right side. X presses his right leg against Y's shoulder to control him, while his left leg is at the ready to apply leverage. X uses his ribs to press down into Y's lungs, preventing Y from turning his body over. Y will be forced to use his hands to resist, either striking or grabbing X in an effort to get up. X takes advantage of Y's desperate movements and grabs Y's right hand with his left. X positions the upper part of Y's right arm over the top of his right leg and then presses downward with his left leg on the lower part of Y's arm. With Y's arm pinched between his legs in this manner, X need only lift his right leg as he presses down with his left to break Y's arm.

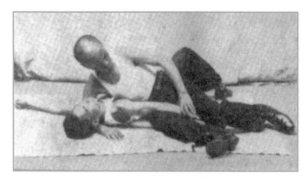

Figure 6-20: Pinching the Elbow

Number Twenty-One: Mounting the Horse

This technique is applied during mortal combat when an opponent has fallen to the ground.

Explanation

X sees that Y has fallen down onto his left side. X takes advantage of the situation and quickly follows Y to the ground. Before Y has a chance to regroup, X grabs Y's right hand with both hands and simultaneously extends his left leg over the top of Y's chest. X sits on Y's right side and presses downward into Y's chest with his left leg. X pulls Y's right arm across the upper part of his leg. X pulls down forcefully with both hands, lifts his right leg, and pushes outward and downward with his left leg. Y's elbow will be broken.

Figure 6-21: Mounting the Horse

Number Twenty-Two: Separating the Arms

This technique is applied in hand-to-hand combat when both fighters have fallen to the ground. You can control and break both your opponent's arms.

Explanation

X sees that Y has fallen to the ground. X follows Y to the ground, straddling Y's chest and pressing his weight down onto Y. Y will have trouble breathing or moving his body and will certainly try to resist by pushing X or grabbing at his throat. X takes advantage of Y's attempts and grabs both of his hands, pulling Y's hands outward to the left and right. At the same time, X squeezes his knees inward against Y's arms with sudden force, breaking Y's elbows.

Figure 6-22: Separating the Arms

Number Twenty-Three: Forcing the Elbow

This technique is applied during hand-to-hand combat when an opponent is already on the ground.

Explanation

X sees that Y has fallen to the ground and quickly takes advantage of the situation to sit astride Y's upper body. In an attempt to resist, Y reaches up with his right hand. X uses his right hand to push Y's right hand to the left side of his neck; he traps Y's hand between his shoulder and neck. At the same time, X hooks both hands behind the point of Y's right elbow and pulls inward and to the right as he pushes forward and to the left with his shoulder. If force is applied suddenly, it will break Y's elbow.

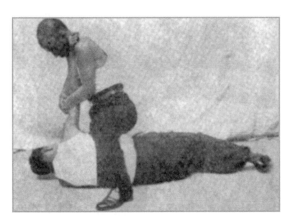

Figure 6-23: Forcing the Elbow

Finger Techniques

Number One: Lifting the Tendon

The following four techniques (Figure 7-1a–Figure 7-1d) are used after you are seized by your opponent. Apply pressure to the opponent's tendons to force him to release his grip and then follow up with offensive techniques.

Explanation

There are three vital points on the back of an opponent's hand. The first point is between the index and middle fingers. The second point is between the middle and ring fingers, and the third point is between the ring and little fingers. In addition to these points, there is a tendon on the back of the hand that crosses the junction of the hand and wrist. If this point is seized, the opponent will relax his hand and you will be able to apply counter techniques. However, in order to apply these grasping techniques, one must undergo a long period of training, greatly developing the strength of the fingers.

When grasping the first point, you should first press forcefully and deeply into the tendon that crosses the outside of the index finger. Then, lift up the tendon at the inside of the middle finger and the opponent will feel numbness in his arm that radiates throughout his body. The opponent will not be able to hold his grip and his hand will relax. See Figure 7-1a.

Figure 7-1a: Lifting the Tendon, Part One

To attack the second point, use the technique in the same manner as described above. In this case, however, the bottom part of the hand must adhere tightly to the opponent's middle finger and dig in deeply as the thumb lifts the tendon above the ring finger. The three points can all be attacked in this manner. See Figure 7-1b.

Figure 7-1b: Lifting the Tendon, Part Two

The Tiger's Mouth point is between the thumb and index finger. When an opponent reaches forward to grab you, counter by grabbing his incoming hand as the thumb of your other hand presses forcefully into the Tiger's Mouth point. The opponent will feel sore and numb, and his hand will relax. See Figure 7-1c.

Figure 7-1c: Pinching the Tiger's Mouth

This variation is also applied as the opponent reaches out to grab you. Grab his wrist with one hand and press the thumb of the other hand between the middle and ring fingers. Press down strongly and lift his tendon upward. The nerves in the opponent's entire arm will become numb and his hand will relax. See Figure 7-1d.

Figure 7-1d: Pressing the Fist

All of the above techniques require extreme speed and precision in order to render an opponent's hand powerless. Improper application will not only be ineffective, but will also allow your opponent to gain the upper hand on you.

Number Two: Pushing the Fingers

This technique is applied when an opponent throws a straight punch. Break his fingers to gain control of him.

Explanation

Y throws a right straight punch at X's chest. X dodges to his left and uses his left hand to grab Y's left wrist. At the same time, X uses his right palm or the fleshy part of his thumb to push Y's thumb downward. X pulls inward and downward with his left hand. Y's thumb will be broken.

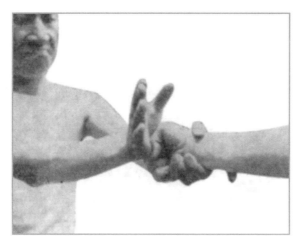

Figure 7-2: Pushing the Fingers

Most people will make a fist by curling their fingers inward and then hooking the thumb over the index and middle fingers. People who close their fists in this manner are easily controlled by fighters who are skilled in seizing and grasping techniques. Of all the various styles of striking, only the flat fist of Tantui and the scorpion fist of Tongbeiquan are hard to control. The flat fist of Tantui is also made by curling the fingers inward, but the thumb is bent and placed below the second knuckle of the index finger, keeping it safely tucked away.

Number Three: Rolling the Fingers

Although the movement of this technique is small, its effect is great. It may be applied at any time.

Explanation

When an opponent reaches forward to grab you, counter by grabbing his fingers; place your thumb above on the top of his hand and your four fingers below. You may grab the opponent's index finger (or any of the other fingers) and press hard to bend the finger inward. The thumb presses forward and downward as the fingers forcefully pull the opponent's finger inward. Your opponent will feel unbearable pain and his finger will be broken. If you feel the opponent may pull his hand free, you can use your left hand to grab the opponent's wrist, preventing his escape. If you do not wish to break the finger, loosen your grip, and maintain control—the opponent will be forced to follow wherever you lead.

Figure 7-3: Rolling the Fingers

Number Four: Leading the Fist

This technique is used to intercept either a chopping attack to the face or an attempt to grab the chest.

Explanation

Y attacks X's face or chest. X quickly uses his right hand to grab the index or middle finger of Y's right hand. X pushes outward with his thumb and pulls inward with his four fingers. X moves his body backward, pulling Y's hand inward and downward as he bends Y's finger backward. Y's finger will be broken.

Figure 7-4: Leading the Fist

Number Five: Separating the Fingers

This technique may be applied to break an opponent's fingers, causing him to lose most of his will to resist. It may also be applied to control a suspect, preventing him from moving freely and forcing him to comply with your orders.

Explanation

X grabs Y's left thumb tightly from below with his left hand; the web of his thumb is pressed firmly into the web of Y's thumb. At the same time, X grabs Y's little and ring fingers in the same manner. X pulls Y's fingers apart to the left and right as he bends them upward. X presses his right elbow forward into the back of Y's left arm, keeping his body pressed tightly against Y's body. X now controls Y and can walk him forward. If need be, X can break Y's fingers.

Figure 7-5: Separating the Fingers

Section **8**

Crotch, Leg, and Foot Techniques

Number One: Lifting the Crotch

This technique is used to counter a grab to the crotch.

Explanation

Y grabs X's crotch with his right hand. X quickly grabs Y's right hand with his left hand and pulls backward while quickly poking Y in the eyes with the index and middle fingers of his right hand (the Swallow Steals the Nest technique). Y will be forced to release his grip. Since the crotch grab is a very dangerous attack, using any other methods of defense will not be quick enough. In this case, using the Lifting the Tendon or Pinching the Tiger's Mouth techniques may not be effective. Quickly apply the Swallow Steals the Nest technique and gouge the opponent's eyes. One may also use the Double Wasps Enter the Ears technique and strike with both hands to the junctions of the opponent's temples and jaw. Use these techniques to control the opponent or the opponent will control you.

Figure 8-1: Lifting the Crotch

Number Two: Breaking the Leg

This technique is applied during hand-to-hand combat to break an opponent's leg and bring him under control.

Explanation

In this scenario, Y is either sitting, lying on the ground, or engaged in ground wrestling with X. Y attempts to apply the scissors technique to X's waist. X wraps his right leg around Y's left upper leg from the bottom and stretches his right leg across Y's stomach, adhering his right foot to Y's right ribs. At the same time, X grabs Y's right arm with both hands and forcefully pulls backward. X uses his left foot to press behind Y's right upper leg. X pushes forcefully with his leg while pulling strongly with his arms as he leans his body backward and turns to the left. X also straightens his right leg with force, causing Y's left leg to break.

Figure 8-2: Breaking the Leg

Number Three: Sitting on the Leg

This technique is applied during a fight to break your opponent's leg.

Explanation

X and Y are locked together, wrestling on the ground. When Y inserts a leg between X's legs, X quickly turns around to sit just above Y's knee. At the same time, X grabs Y's foot with both hands and pulls upward forcefully as he leans his body backward, pushing down with his rear end. A sudden application of force will break Y's knee.

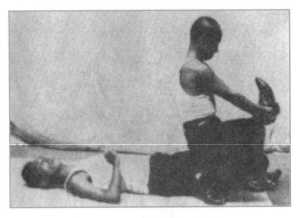

Figure 8-3: Sitting on the Leg

Number Four: Stamping the Leg

This technique is applied after you lose your balance and fall to the ground, allowing you to turn defeat into victory.

Explanation

Y sees that X has fallen to the ground. Y steps up with his right foot and strikes with a downward hammer blow to X's head. X props himself up on his right elbow and grabs Y's wrist with his left hand. X then forcefully pulls Y down as he simultaneously hooks the top of his right foot behind Y's right heel. X forcefully kicks Y in the knee with his left leg in coordination with the backward pull on Y's arm. Y will fall back and down onto the ground. X can now follow up with other techniques. X may also kick Y's knee with a sudden and forceful blow in order to break his leg. Note that this technique may also be applied without first grabbing your opponent's hand.

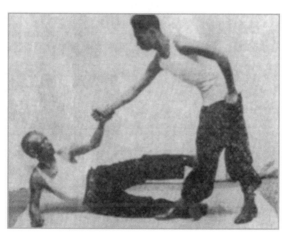

Figure 8-4: Stamping the Leg

Number Five: Breaking the Foot

This technique is applied when an opponent kicks from a standing position or kicks from the ground.

Explanation

Y is on the ground kicking up at X with his left foot. X grabs Y's foot with both hands and pinches it with his right armpit, squeezing it forcefully with his right upper arm. X then bends his right arm and reaches below Y's leg to grab the lower part of his own left arm. X forcefully presses his left hand downward on the top of Y's shin. X leans his body backward while pressing forward and upward. Y's ankle will be broken.

Figure 8-5: Breaking the Foot

About the Translator

TIM CARTMELL began his martial arts training with the Chinese styles, including ten years of study in China. He is an Asian Full-Contact fighting champion, a submissions grappling champion, two-time Pan American Brazilian Jiu Jitsu champion, and seven-time winner of the Copa Pacifica de Jiu Jitsu. Cartmell holds an eighth-degree black belt in Kung Fu San Soo, is a lineage holder in several Chinese internal martial arts styles, and holds a black belt in Brazilian jiu jitsu.

He is the author of *Effortless Combat Throws;* co-author of *Passing the Guard* and *Xing Yi Nei Gong: Xing Yi Health Maintenance and Strength Development;* and the translator of *Practical Chin Na, A Study of Taijiquan, The Method of Chinese Wrestling,* and *The Method of Chin Na.* He is also featured in *Nei Jia Quan: Internal Martial Arts.*

Cartmell teaches at the Shen Wu Academy of Martial Arts in Garden Grove, California.

www.shenwu.com